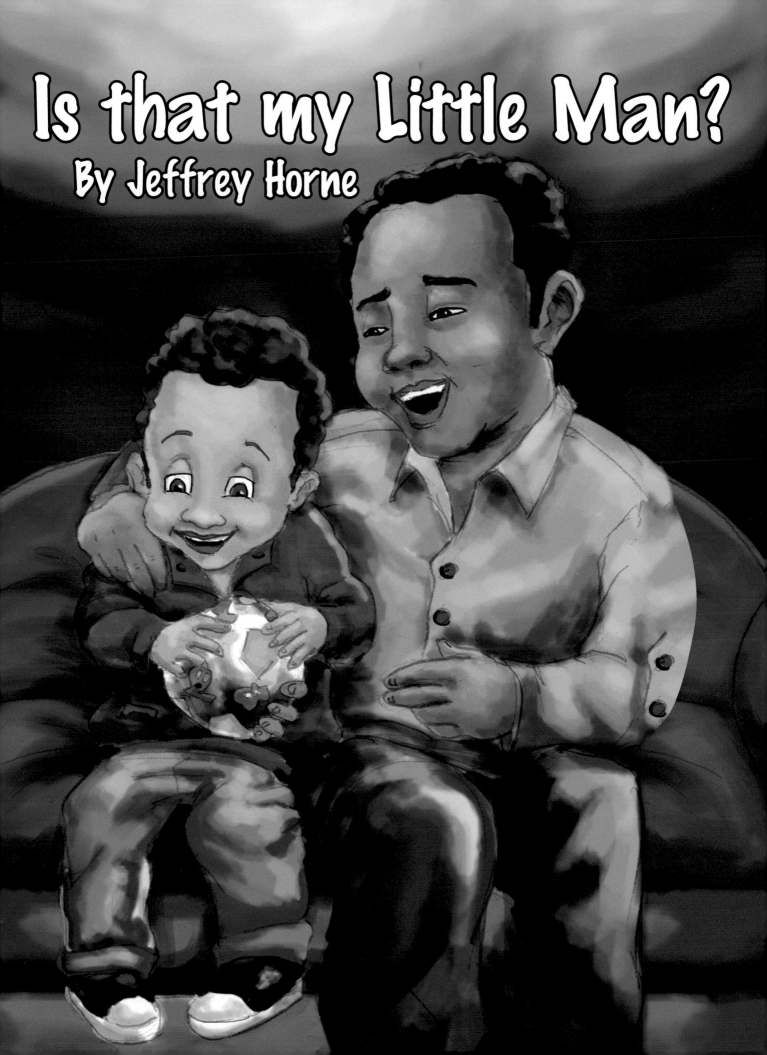

Is that my Little Man?

By Jeffrey Horne

To order additional copies of this book, contact:
Xlibris
844-714-8691
www.Xlibris.com
Orders@Xlibris.com

ISBN: Softcover   978-1-6698-2835-8
        EBook   978-1-6698-2834-1

Print information available on the last page

Rev. date: 06/08/2022

I would like to dedicate the book to my father Hubert S. Horne, my mother Maxine D. Horne and my brother Elias Horne for their loving support. To Ryqui, for your inspiration and for everything that you do for me and our son. Thank you all family and friends.

The book is also dedicated to the loving memory of:

Annie Clea Fox
Haywood T. Fox Jr.
Anthony D. Alexander Jr.

IS THAT MY
LITTLE MAN
BRUSHING HIS TEETH?

IS THAT MY LITTLE MAN EATING HIS BREAKFAST?

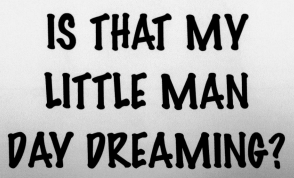

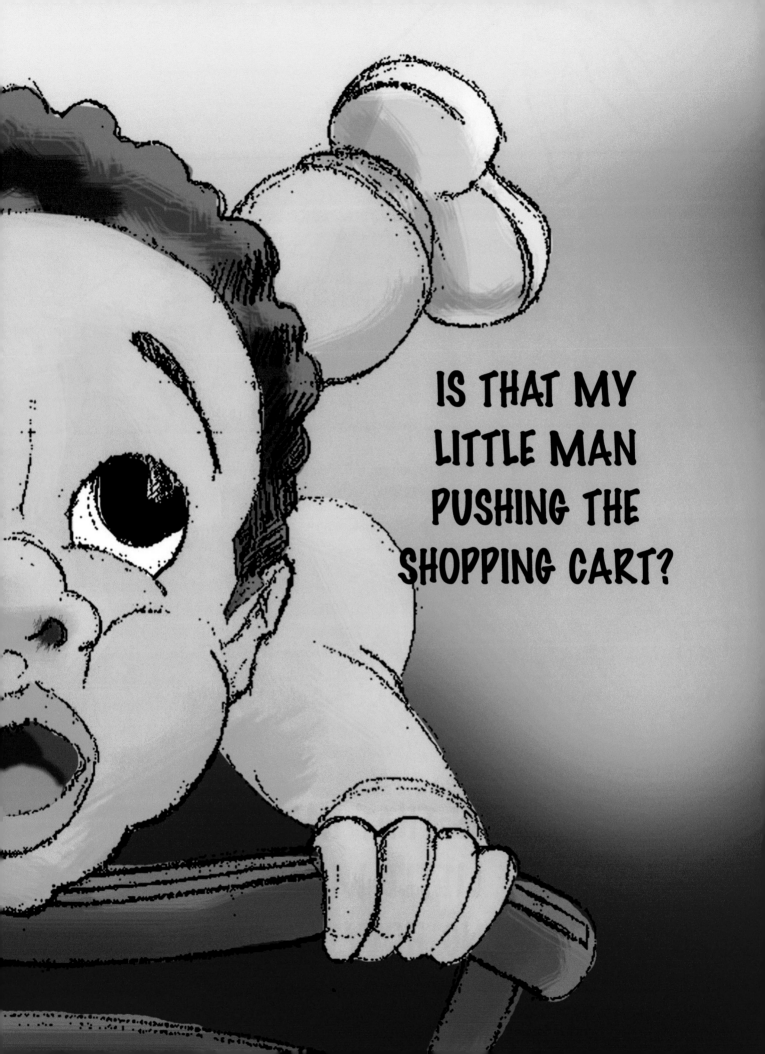

IS THAT MY
LITTLE MAN
LEARNING HOW TO WALK?

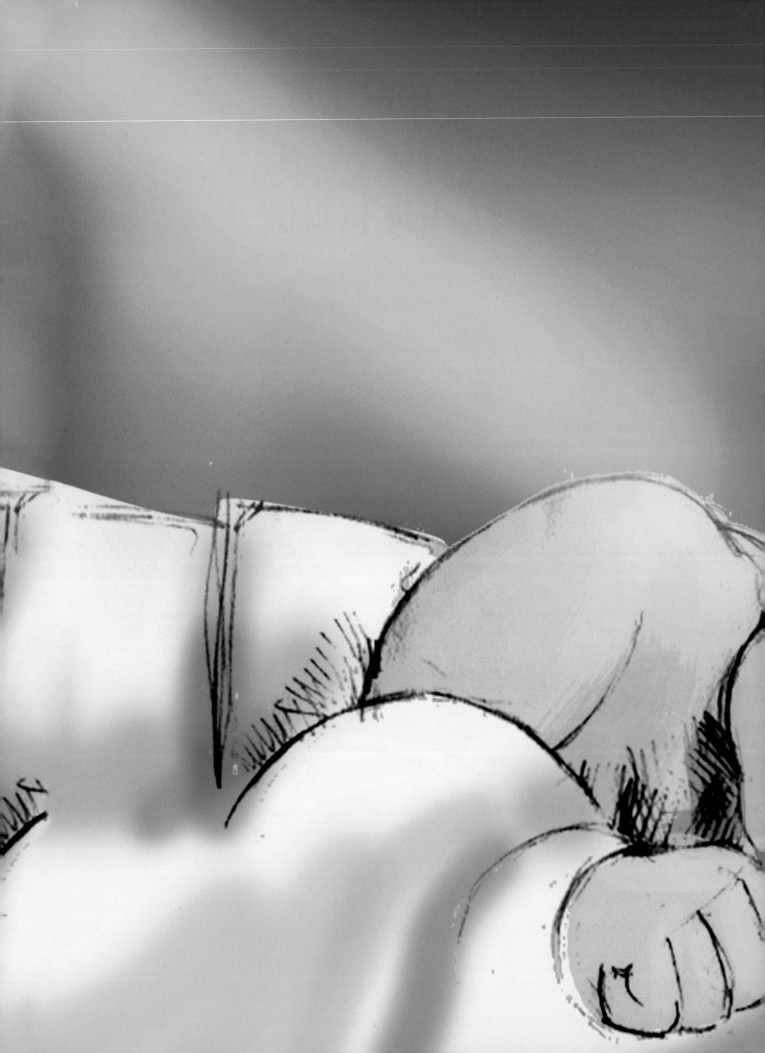

Printed in the United States
by Baker & Taylor Publisher Services

by Baker & Taylor Publisher Services